C000185860

PiXZ PEOPLE
Little Books of Great Lives

LAWRENCE
OF ARABIA

RODNEY LEGG

First published in Great Britain in 2010

Copyright text © 2010 Rodney Legg.
Contemporary photography by Rodney Legg and Maggie & Tony Radcliffe

All rights reserved. No part of this publication may be reproduced,
stored in a retrieval system, or transmitted in any form or by any
means without the prior permission of the copyright holder.

British Library Cataloguing-in-Publication Data
A CIP record for this title is available from the British Library

ISBN 978 1 906887 88 9

PiXZ Books
Halsgrove House, Ryelands Industrial Estate,
Bagley Road, Wellington, Somerset TA21 9PZ
Tel: 01823 653777
Fax: 01823 216796
email: sales@halsgrove.com

An imprint of Halstar Ltd, part of the Halsgrove group of companies
Information on all Halsgrove titles is available at: www.halsgrove.com

Printed and bound in China by Toppan Leefung Printing Ltd

Contents

*Captain Lawrence of the Intelligence Corps
with personalised head-dress in Cairo.*

The Lawrence brothers (left to right) – Ned, Frank, Arnie, Bob and Will – at Oxford in 1910.

A Tale of Two Families

Though illegitimate, Thomas Edward Lawrence, came from gentrified Anglo-Irish stock, originating in Hinckley, Leicestershire. His father, Thomas Robert Tighe Chapman, was nephew and cousin to two childless male heirs of Sir Benjamin Chapman, baronet, of South Hill, Delvin, County Westmeath. He could claim ancestry from Sir Walter Raleigh and inherited a land title going back to Oliver Cromwell. Thomas Chapman's mother, Louisa Vansittart, was the grand-daughter of the 1st Lord Auckland. Tall and bearded, Thomas Chapman married his cousin Edith Sarah Hamilton Boyd, the daughter of the late George Augustus Rochfort-Boyd, High Sheriff of Westmeath, in 1873.

Thomas Lawrence's pursuits, such as riding, snipe-shooting, and yachting, were standard for a Victorian country gentleman. With wife Edith he had four daughters but there was a gulf in the relationship. She was a humourless harridan who evangelised the tenantry. Her reputation extended to Dublin — the 'City of Sin' — where to Catholics she was the 'Holy Viper'. She seldom went there, however, and for most of the time the sternest of values were reserved to the marital home. Misdemeanours indoors were punished by humiliating punishments such as a chamber-pot being tied around the neck of one the girls. 'Contamination' was an offence that caused containment with the guilty girl being locked in her room for five days at a stretch and given only bread and water.

Thomas turned to drink and the children's nanny. Sarah Junner, a petite lass with an English mother and Norwegian father, was born in Sunderland on 31 August 1861. Brought up by an aunt and uncle, an Anglican minister in Scotland, she came to Westmeath with the impeccable references of 'a true daughter of God'. One day in 1884, nanny and master were overheard talking intimately, and the resultant schism ruptured residual relations between Edith and Thomas.

He walked out and took Sarah with him. They sailed to Holyhead under assumed names – Thomas Lawrence and Sarah Maden – and set up home in Tremadoc, Snowdonia, as Mr and Mrs Thomas Lawrence. Just as Edith had given him girls, Sarah produced boys. The first was Montagu Robert 'Bob' Lawrence in December 1885. The second, born in the night of 15-16 August 1888, was Thomas Edward 'Ned' Lawrence. William George 'Will' Lawrence followed on 10 December 1889.

Family life was hardly settled. Sarah, like Edith, became drawn to Oxford Movement Anglicanism and was strictly tee-total, as well as being the disciplinarian of the house, beating the boys on their bare buttocks, not gratuitously but most frequently to Ned. For a couple of years the Lawrences moved around in an extended triangle that had its corners at Harlech,

St Helier and Douglas, Isle of Man (where Thomas Tighe Chapman could be closer to his bankers and release funds to his first family).

From St Helier they moved to Dinant in France in 1890 so that the boys could attend Freres School and its twice-weekly gymnastic classes for expatriates. The family returned to Jersey for Frank Helier Lawrence to be born with British nationality on 7 February 1893. The next move was to England, in the spring of 1894, to Langley Lodge, opposite St Francis Church at Blackfield, Hampshire.

The New Forest began at the end of the track and Lepe Road on the other side of the hedge headed for the Solent in a mile.

> 'In the long history of the College no member has attracted so much comment and controversy as Lawrence; none has merited greater appreciation.'
> J. N. L. Baker of Jesus College, Oxford.

Its view across to Cowes and the world's classiest yachts became Thomas Lawrence's delight. On the Isle of Wight in 1895, attending church at Ryde, Thomas and Sarah heard visiting preacher Canon Alfred Christopher, charismatic rector of St Aldate's at Oxford.

This influenced their decision, in 1896, to move to 2 Polstead Road, Oxford, where Arnold Walter 'Arnie' Lawrence was born on 2 May 1900. The boys attended City of Oxford High School where the headmaster was Arthur Wilson Cave and assistant master Revd Ernest Cox. The latter remembered the 'band of brothers'. Bob was 'conscientious and kind'. Ned 'self-possessed, purposeful, inscrutable ... self-reliant'. Will, the 'one beautiful to look upon', was grave. Dressed identically, in blue-and-white striped jerseys, they went off together on their bicycles in a line with 'the eldest in front and the youngest last'.

Above and below: *The Lawrence family home at No. 2 Polstead Road, Oxford.*

The blue plaque above the front door to No. 2.

Pre-war excavations at Carchemish, for the British Museum, provided cover to monitor construction of the Berlin to Baghdad Railway, which headed straight towards the world's biggest oilfield at Basra on the Persian Gulf.

Ned regularly went to lectures at Oxford Archaeological Society and cycled across the country to visit mediaeval castles and take rubbings of monumental brasses. He picked up pottery and other artefacts from development sites, notably the city's Civet Cat hostelry, and presented them to the Ashmolean Museum. In 1906, when he was 16, he reached his adult height of 5 feet 5 inches, as measured and marked beside the door to a downstairs cupboard. The outward sign that he was different from his brothers and separate from the rest of the family — literally — was that a two-room brick and tile 'Summer-house' was built for him at the bottom of Polstead Road garden.

Ned nearly won a scholarship to St John's College and then

The 'Summer-house' built for T. E. Lawrence in the Polstead Road garden.

gained a subsidised 'history exhibition' for Welsh-born students, to enter Jesus College, Oxford, in 1907. Castle tours extended to continental Europe and then, in June 1909, aboard the Peninsular & Oriental steamship *Mongolia*, to Port Said. From there he went to Beirut and Damascus, in search of the Crusader castles of Syria, and returned to Oxford in 1910 to collect a first class degree in history.

By the end of the year, Ned was back in the Middle East with a British Museum expedition to dig at Carchemish, a Hittite lost city on the Euphrates. Lawrence learnt photography and surveying as he picked up a working knowledge of Arabic. He went off into Arabia between periods of excavation and occasional visits to England. The contemporary backdrop, of 'horrible political complots', became apparent in 1913, and archaeology provided a convenient cover for military map-making. This was confirmed by David Garnett when he edited Lawrence's letters:

'For the archaeological survey which he and Woolley were asked to carry out for the Palestine Exploration Fund had been designed by Lord Kitchener as a piece of camouflage for a survey by Captain [Stewart] Newcombe, Royal Engineers, completing one he had made himself as a young man. And the territory involved had

Top: *Salim Ahmed – known as Dahoum – dressed in Lawrence's clothes at Carchemish before the Great War*
Bottom: *Lawrence posing in Dahmoum's clothes during the Carchemish excavations.*

already given rise to a serious incident between England and Turkey.'

That incident, in 1906, enabled Egypt to annexe the Sinai peninsula and 'was hailed as a triumph for Sir Edward Grey's diplomacy'. Wilfrid Blunt, however, warned that it would rupture relations with Turkey – which happened with catastrophic consequences – namely the alliance between Constantinople and Berlin during the Great War.

Back in the United Kingdom, Sir Benjamin Rupert Tighe Chapman died on 22 March 1914 and his cousin – Lawrence's father –

inherited the title as Sir Thomas Robert Tighe Chapman, the 7th baronet in a line from 1782. No address appeared in *Who's Who* where he remained married to Edith (with four daughters). Because he lacked a legitimate male heir — thereby excluding Bob — the title became extinct when Thomas died on 8 April 1919. One presumes all the boys were aware of the great family secret, if only because Ned knew it, as he confirmed to Charlotte Shaw:

'They thought always they were living in sin, and that we would some day find out. Whereas I knew before I was ten.'

Visiting and describing a chain of 36 Crusader castles across Ottoman Palestine, Lebanon and Syria, in 1909, ensured that Lawrence would be Oxford's undergraduate of the year in 1910.

Four of the five boys were of an age for going to war from 4 August 1914. For two it was end of story. Serving with the Gloucestershire Regiment, on the Western Front, Frank expressed disgust that Ned had sent home photographs of dead Turks.

'I cannot imagine what he did it for. I could get plenty here if I had a camera and wanted to. The human body after death is a most vile and loathsome thing. The one I helped to pull out of the ditch at the last trench but one absolutely defies description.'

Days later, on 9 May 1915, Frank was killed leading an advance in the Battle of Aubers Ridge. Will was shot down over St Quentin on 23 October 1915, just a week after arrival in France, in the first combat loss for newly-formed 13 Squadron of the Royal Flying Corps.

The War in the Desert

Talent-spotted by Colonel Coote Hedley of the War Office, in November 1914, Second Lieutenant Thomas Edward Lawrence left London for 'special service' in the Military Intelligence Office in Cairo. Slovenly dress and eccentric behaviour was offset by his perceptive reports on Arab nationalism. His elevation to the Arab Bureau in the Savoy Hotel, Cairo, under Colonel Gilbert Clayton, reached its full potential in 1916 after the arrival from Oxford of his mentor Lieutenant-Commander David Hogarth — already his surrogate 'father' — with bags of gold sovereigns for Lawrence to go and buy off a rebellion in the Hejaz and then turn the uprising against the Turks.

Adopting the robes of the rank of an Emir came naturally to Lawrence, though he was by no means the first British officer to dress as an Arab. In Mesopotamia, Major Gerard Evelyn Leachman (1880-1920) did so to slip into an enemy redoubt in the Dujaila Depression — to find it manned by only forty sleeping Turks — on the night of 7 March 1916. Meanwhile, Husayn ibn-Ali fired the first shot of the Arab Revolt out of the window of his home in Mecca, at the nearby Turkish barracks, in 1916.

Lawrence's resources escalated from £50 in 1916 to £20,000 the following summer, and rose to £200,000 in 1918 — leading to his Arab nickname, Abu Khayyal ('Father of the

The Oriental Secretary at the British Agency in Cairo, Ronald Storrs, adopted Lawrence and protected his protégé from accusations that he was 'utterly careless of his dress'.

Captain Lawrence (left) and his senior officer,
Lieutenant-Commander David Hogarth (centre),
at the Arab Bureau in Cairo.

Right: *'Sheikh Lawrence' in his*
robes as a Prince of Mecca.

Horseman') because the coins featured an equestrian St George. Allied-supporting Hejazi Arabs were also provided with their own set of stamps — philately being the outward symbol of nationhood — after Ronald Storrs and Lawrence trawled the Islamic Museum for suitable graphics. 'Little Lawrence, my super-cerebral companion,' Storrs called a freshly promoted Major Lawrence.

General Sir Edmund Allenby was less sure and remained puzzled by the conundrum of whether Lawrence the performer was the cloak for Lawrence the charlatan. The world was yet to have a view on the matter. That came about after the fall of Jerusalem, when Lieutenant-General Storrs, as the Military Governor, decided it was time to tell the press. What he had in mind were a few well-placed broadsheet articles by one of David Hogarth's stable of Oxford academics, fellow intelligence officer Harry Pirie-Gordon.

What came to pass, however, was sensational by the standards of the day. International presentation, in the new

Lawrence of Arabia, by Augustus John, in 1919.

media of the newsreels, came courtesy American journalist Lowell Jackson Thomas (1892-1981). Bankrolled by twenty Chicago financiers, he had been commissioned by President Wilson to record the Great War on film, 'as an historical record'. Thomas and his movie cameraman, Harry Chase, had already been attached to armies across Europe from France to the Balkans and were desperate for excitement beyond the carnage.

Colonel John Buchan arranged what became their circuitous and tedious trip through the Middle East — via Cairo, the Nile, Sudan and the Red Sea —

Lieutenant-Colonel Thomas Edward Lawrence of the post-war British Army.

but when the weary travellers arrived in Jerusalem they immediately struck gold. They were met by Lawrence, gilded and jewelled as a Sharif of Mecca. General Allenby consented to them filming at Aqaba and a chivalrous and glamorised version of events captured the public imagination. It was an antidote to reality on the Western Front. Lowell Thomas said of Lawrence:

'Along with his other magnificent talents, he had a rare gift for "backing into the limelight".'

A more considered word-picture of Lawrence was penned by his cousin, Lord Vansittart:

'Lawrence's orders were directions, and he cared nothing about saluting, except that he preferred to dispense with it.'
Driver S. C. Rolls of the
Royal Army Service Corps, 1917.

'Above all, romance was being revived in a khaki world by an unlikely excavator from Carchemish, slim, fair-haired, inexperienced, and a considerable farceur. During the

previous year a rising had broken out against the Turks in the Hejaz. Lawrence helped to spread it with his gift for propaganda — note the tool again — and guerrilla warfare. He and others, more frequent but less famed, blew bridges, wrecked trains, damaged the artery of the Hejaz Railway, reached Aqaba, raided here and there. Some of his feats were exaggerated, for he appealed to imagination, including his own, and seldom appealed in vain. In the Lawrence legend the boundaries between fact and fiction were undemarcated as dunes; but behind the bravura lay bravery, and immense physical stamina behind the frail physique. Gorge-raising ferocity was shown by both Arabs and Turks, above all by the Bedouin.

'. . . Lawrence was always having his biography written, and filled it with flourishes better forgotten for the sake of the rest. Father thought him probably "a rum 'un". He was, but most people are bad actors, and El-Ourens was good. Without that talent he could never have led his Arabs, a poor lot, patchy in courage, ferocious in looting.

It is amusing to compare the enthusiasm worked up for their exploits with our contempt for the Turks. Now the Arabs have displayed their defects, while the Turks have evolved into the mainstay of the Middle East.'

Lawrence wrote to his friend Vyvyan Richards on 15 July 1918:

'You want apparently some vivid colouring of an Arab costume, or of a flying Turk, and we have it all, for that is part of the mise en scene of the successful raider, and hitherto I am that. My bodyguard of 50 Arab tribesmen, picked riders from the young men of the deserts, are more splendid than a tulip garden, and we ride like lunatics and with our Bedouins pounce on unsuspecting Turks and destroy them in heaps: and it is all very gory and nasty after we close grips. I love the preparation, and the journey, and loathe the physical fighting. Disguises, and prices on one's head, and fancy exploits are all part of the pose: how to reconcile it with the Oxford pose I do not know.'

The least reliable account of Lawrence's life is usually his own. He claimed to have crossed enemy territory to Damascus — listing hundreds of places in a 'skeleton diary' — in the fortnight after 4 June, but those he 'met' had no recollection of the encounter and others mustering Arab forces insisted he was with them in Auda abu Tayi's oasis at Nebk. The classic action of the Arab Revolt followed in July 1917 with the capture of the strategic town of Aqaba, at the inland end of the arm of the Red Sea jutting into the Holy Land. Lawrence was in harness as the action started, at Abu'l Lissan on the ridge above Aqaba, and took part waving a revolver as Auda led the crucial charge, but managed to shoot his camel through the head and was found lying comatose on the ground after the Arabs had narrowly won the day. The Turks had been expecting an attack from the sea. Instead the Arabs rushed

'As public sympathy is desirable, we must try and enlist on our side a favourable press.'
Lawrence, writing home, after the capture of Aqaba.

Lawrence on camelback at Aqaba.

Lawrence at a Bedouin camp during the Arab Revolt.

'He still looks absurdly boyish for twenty-nine.'
David Hogarth at Gaza in November 1917
when the French awarded Lawrence
the Croix de Guerre.

their outposts from the north and swept down to the beach. Lawrence took the credit, in descriptions worthy of the Victoria Cross, if another British officer had witnessed events.

On one key date when he was in Aqaba, on 21 November 1917, to accompany Lieutenant-Colonel Pierce Joyce up Wadi Yutm, Lawrence claimed to have been on an espionage mission behind enemy lines, when he was captured and flogged by soldiers in Deraa on the command of Hajim, the Turkish Bey.

The final contributions of the Arab Army began on 8 August 1918 when they turned inland and took Medawera on the Hejaz Railway, with the capture of 120 Turks, two field guns and three machine guns. On 16 September they destroyed a bridge and tore up the railway line 15 miles south of Deraa. Major Lawrence was promoted Lieutenant-Colonel early in 1918. The Arab Army numbered 8,000 and were now a powerful distraction for the Turks on their eastern flank. They expected an attack from Kasr el Azrak towards Deraa and Damascus.

Another hero, Colonel Richard Meinhertzhagen who headed Allenby's Intelligence Corps unit, convinced the Turks that this was the plan, by dropping a brief-case in the street, whilst pretending to have been shot. Among genuine contents was a fabricated document about an attack from the desert. This stratagem was a brilliant success and enabled Allenby to prepare an offensive above the Mediterranean with three mounted divisions and 383 guns. The presence of a force on this scale remained unknown to the Turkish headquarters. It

Tulip bomb sabotage to the Turks' Hejaz railway.

was therefore with complete surprise that the coastal forces attacked at dawn on 18 September and broke through double lines of Turkish trenches. Inland, the Arabs took Deraa on 27 September, and headed immediately for Damascus which they entered on 1 October 1918, just ahead of Australian cavalry. Lawrence, Huseyn ibn-Ali and Nuri al-Said followed, to carry out an instant coup in which they took it upon themselves to appoint Shukry Pasha as 'military governor'. Allenby and Prince Feisal entered the Syrian capital two days later.

Lawrence, personally, was grief stricken with personal loss. Salim Ahmed, known as Dahoum ('The Dark One') had been Lawrence's 'donkey boy' when he was excavating at Carchemish, in 1911 and 1912. 'He wrestles beautifully, better than all of his age and size,' Lawrence wrote. The

*Lawrence at the front of a Rolls-Royce tender, at the head
of the Arab Army, entering Damascus on 1 October 1918.*

General Sir Edmund Allenby (in the back seat with Lady Allenby) led the Egyptian Expeditionary Force.

General Sir Edmund Allenby, Commander-in-Chief, taking the salute at a victory fly-past in Palestine.

brown-eyed lad captivated Lawrence. They swapped clothes in order to photograph each other, with the association turning into a complete cultural exchange when Lawrence brought Dahoum to London and Oxford, for the summer of 1913. During the war they were together again, and though Lawrence had risked the youth to spy around Turkish positions it was to typhoid that he lost him, on the road to Damascus in September 1918. 'I loved that boy,' Lawrence told Tom Beamont, the machine-gunner on his armoured car. Salim

Ahmed, arguably, is the 'S.A.' of the dedication in *The Seven Pillars of Wisdom*.

Returning from Palestine, en route in a Handley Page transport aircraft between Paris and Lyons, Lawrence wrote the following note in the back of his copy of Robert Vansittart's *The Singing Caravan*, now in the Bodleian Library:

> *'I wrought for him freedom to lighten his sad eyes: but he had died waiting for me. So I threw my gift away and now not anywhere will I find rest and peace.'*

Lawrence later confirmed the Arab link in a letter to his 'humane banker' Robin Buxton:

> *'S.A. was a person, now dead, regard for whom lay behind my labour for the Arabic peoples. I do not propose to go further into detail thereupon.'*

For Arab nationalism, too, Damascus was an illusory triumph.

Lawrence saw Prince Feisal as the head of what was now rapidly being transformed into a British sphere of influence, as he told Richard Meinertzhagen:

'My own ambition is that the Arabs should be our first brown dominion.'

What the Arabs won in war was soon prised from them through diplomacy. Sir Robert Vansittart, the principal civil servant at the Foreign Office between the wars, summed up the deceptions that lay behind the Paris Conference:

'Arabs and their Lawrence held us pledged to the United States of Arabia with its capital at Damascus – an exaggeration, but everyone exaggerated. We did not, could not, tell them that by the Sykes-Picot agreement of May 1916 – concluded behind the backs of the Italians and Sherif of Mecca – we had covenanted with the French for the partition of Asia Minor and the Arab parts of ex-Sublime Porte by allotting Mesopotamia to ourselves,

> To the Strand Magazine – promoting Lowell Thomas's articles – Lawrence had become *'a great white god'* who *'was the uncrowned King of the Hejaz, Prince of Mecca'.*

Cilicia and Syria to the French, and other slices to other people including ex-Holy Russia now cancelled. Symmetrically we had not told the French of our promises to the Arabs, who had anyhow got into Damascus in October.'

Vansittart did not hear anyone mention Article 22 of the League of Nations Covenant which stipulated 'that the wishes of these communities must be a principal consideration in the selection of the Mandatory'. In April 1920, the League announced the 'Mandates' for Syria and Lebanon (France), and Mesopotamia and Palestine (Britain). Nobody was 'mad enough' to want the mandate for Armenia. 'Gentlemen, after all, what stands between us?' someone asked. A voice piped up:

'Only a million dead Armenians.'

The diplomat Aubrey Herbert MP of Pixton Park, Dulverton, who had served in the Dardanelles and Mesopotamia, was adamant that Lawrence had said it. Lawrence said it was Herbert, which failed to convince Robert Graves:

'But Herbert was pro-Turk, and it was a TE-ish remark.'

Everyone was unhappy with the outcome. The Jews wanted more, and Arthur Balfour gave in with a statement that promised 'a national home for the Jewish people' but with a caveat that was impossible to honour, 'it being understood that nothing shall be done which may prejudice the civil and religious rights of existing non-Jewish communities in Palestine'. In response there were anti-Jewish riots in Jerusalem and a separate insurrection among the Iraqis. Lawrence flew home to England and went to Buckingham Palace on 30 October 1918 to tell King George V personally why he was refusing both the Companion of the Bath and

Distinguished Service Order honours which had been gazetted. He felt the Arabs had been betrayed by the Sykes-Picot Agreement and said he was quite prepared to fight the French for the recovery of Syria (though His Majesty was left thinking that he was threatening to fight the British as well).

Lord Vansittart was emphatic in demolishing a claim by Lawrence that he was offered the post of High Commissioner of Egypt and the Sudan in 1922 (and again in 1924):

'There is no truth in Lawrence's intimation that the job was offered to him. Even less substance is in his claim to have had the chance in 1922. The appointment lay with Curzon. If Winston [Churchill] had ever foolishly proposed Lawrence, I should have heard, for Curzon would have laughed him out of court, and the laughter would not have been kind. Still more untruthful is the suggestion that anyone ever thought seriously of pushing out Maurice Hankey to let in Lawrence as Secretary of the Cabinet. Lawrence would have been fantastic in any high

Lawrence in suit and tie (top right) with Colonial Secretary Winston Churchill (front, third from left) at the Cairo Conference which re-shaped the Middle East in 1921.

officialdom. Montagu Norman was mad enough to want the Prince of Mecca for Secretary of the Bank of England. Everyone was indeed potty about this flood-lit man, who deserved his Bath and Distinguished Service Order but nothing like apotheosis. What a gifted pair of poseurs Monty and TE would have made! But what Clemenceau said about Klotz and addition might have been muttered of the Prince by the clerks.'

Sojourn in Epping Forest

Lawrence's lifelong friend and fellow Jesus College graduate Vyvyan Warren Richards, a history master at Bancroft's School, Woodford Green, moved into a cabin on top of Pole Hill, Chingford, in 1912. Having established a youth cadet camp for 'Pioneers' in the Warren — with Epping Forest on the other side of the fence — he approached Lawrence for support. This was forthcoming:

'Yes, the Epping scheme: a superb idea. I was beginning to have a fear that we were putting the hut before the press so to speak. Is it possible in any way to use the roof-beams of the Hall near Jesus? I mean those now stored in Oxford for us. There is a fair amount, and the king-posts are lovely things. Sail in, and carry out all to your content and I will be more than acquiescent.'

The oak beams had been salvaged from a demolished stable-block beside Jesus College. Though Richards espoused the arts and crafts ideals of William Morris the aesthetic regime became increasingly para-military as the world went to war. Boys made their own Crusader-style silver lapel badges, took a cold bath each day, went on long treks, played at being mediaeval knights, acted out sagas and slept in a bell tent. Richards recalled that Lawrence paid them visits whenever he was back in the country:

'There was one characteristic visit when he came to the school where I taught and was told he would find me in the woods across the way with some of the boys. It was a winter night, with snow upon the ground and trees, and the moon shining upon their whiteness. We had filled a bell tent with brushwood covered with rugs, and flung the

guys [ropes] *on each side of the door back till half the tent was open. Before us a great fire blazed with the background of snow-clad trees behind it. So we sat there toasting and telling tales. Presently a silent figure came quietly round the corner and joined us. He, too, had tales to tell of other young-minded folk about camp-fires. It was like his natural simpleness to join us and be content there; and after to walk and talk in the woods with me, content again with the simple fare my mind offered him.'*

The camp was initially located beside Knighton Wood, Woodford Green, on land owned by open spaces champion Edward North Buxton. An anti-aircraft battery was established nearby on the Pole Hill viewpoint to fire at German Zeppelin airships. On 1 September 1919, Lawrence wrote to Richards:

'I'm out of the Army today; and today I have paid for 5 acres 2 roods 30 poles of Pole Hill: that is the whole upper field down to the rudimentary hedge. I haven't got the conveyance so am not yet the legal owner, but they cannot

draw back on the bargain, and so far as I'm concerned is finished ... I have not yet been able to buy the hedge from Chingford [Rise] *Estates, and am so short of funds temporarily that I'm not pressing them vigorously.'*

The field was acquired from Revd W. E Moll, by deeds dated 19 September 1919, and Lawrence proceeded to enlarge his holding by purchasing eight interlocking plots, covering 18 acres of Pole Hill. This jigsaw was completed on 22 March 1923 with land partly owned by Arthur Bowmar Portar who was the art master at Bancroft's School. Meanwhile, however, Richards's wooden hut — the Warren — had been destroyed by a grass fire during the heatwave of 1921. Lawrence was possessive about the loss when he wrote to Eric Kennington from the Grand Continental Hotel, Cairo, on 1 October:

'My house in Epping has burnt down.'

His family home, in Oxford, had just been sold and Lawrence's personal library was at Pole Hill. It survived the fire, stored nearby in a hut left over from the wartime gun battery on the east side of the summit. Two old 'dust-eroded' teak doors were en route to Pole Hill from Jedda. These were acquired on 8 July 1921 when Lawrence was negotiating with King Hussein on behalf of the British Government.

Richards and his boys immediately threw their energies into recovering from the setback on the nearby viewpoint:

'My burnt-down hut was replaced, with the help of a camp of boy volunteers from the school, by a cloister and garden and diving pool, which became rather beautiful and pleasant by the time Lawrence seriously contemplated settling on the hill with me. Seven miles of virgin forest lapped its boundaries, ending there; and London lay spread beneath.'

The Cloister, built by Lawrence's friend Vyvyan Richards, on Corporation of London land.

Something more ambitious was being planned. The leading South African architect (Sir) Herbert Baker agreed to draw up preliminary designs for Lawrence to build a pre-Raphaelite Hall, in the image of William Morris's Burgstead, above Richards's 'Cloister' on the 300-feet summit. Lawrence contemplated setting up a private press in this Utopia, to produce *The Seven Pillars of Wisdom*, while blithely ignoring what to others were insurmountable access difficulties.

In the event, however, the lives of both Lawrence and Richards moved in different directions. Lawrence enlisted in the RAF as John Hume Ross in August 1922. About this time something happened between Vyvyan Richards and Bancroft's School, causing the teacher to quit his post, and leave for South Wales. He remained one of Lawrence's closest friends

The Cloister and its pond were taken over by the 1st Highams Park Rover Scouts. Lawrence's books remained stored in the nearby ex-military hut on Pole Hill until 1928.

Then Lawrence did the right thing for the land and its setting by rejecting a £7,000 offer from developers and conveying it instead to the Conservators of Epping Forest in 1930. He asked only the same price as he had paid for it. The £4,450 payment came direct to him from Chingford Urban District Council which in turn took roadside strips to bring adjoining streets up to standard. Suburbia was brought to a stop behind Pole Hill Road, Woodberry Way, Connaught Avenue and Forest View, each with

Lawrence's plaque on the obelisk to Regency astronomer John Pond.

access into the land. Lawrence's 18 acres shrank in the process, according to the council's minutes, to 13.25 acres of public open space.

The pantiled-roofed Cloister survives and is still in use by a charity group. The site of its predecessor — called the Warren — lies just below the trees on the grassy plateau. The location and its history has been researched by Maggie Radcliffe of Waltham Abbey. Its present landmarks are an Ordnance Survey triangulation pillar and a stubby obelisk dating from 1824 which commemorates a local worthy, Revd John Pond (1767-1836), who was appointed Astronomer Royal in 1811 and compiled a list of 1,113 stars published in 1833.

Greenwich Observatory can be seen from the spot and its meridian line of longitude passes 19 feet to the east of the pillar. The Warren stood 60 feet to the south of the obelisk. Guy Osborne, the conservation officer for Waltham Forest, with Mr and Mrs Tony Radcliffe and Rae Woods unveiled an additional plaque on the pillar, commemorating the Lawrence connection, on 29 April 2008.

Returns to Uniform

Though entitled *With Allenby in Palestine*, Lowell Thomas's film lecture centred on the 'strange story of Colonel Thomas Lawrence'. It filled the Albert Hall and went on to run at the Covent Garden Theatre through 1919. Meanwhile, Lieutenant-Colonel Lawrence was given a fellowship and rooms at All Souls College to return to 'the blessed peace and quiet days of Oxford', though escaping notoriety was hardly helped by a prank in which he flew the flag of the Hijaz from one of the pinnacles. For a real retreat, he preferred the attic above the architect's office of Sir Herbert Baker at 14 Barton Street, Westminster.

> 'Lawrence was one of the few men I have ever known who did not know what fear was.'
> – Lieutenant-Colonel Archibald Donald Strange-Boston RE.

He stripped for the next phase of his life by posing for Lady Kennet — the widow of Captain Robert Falcon Scott — who sculpted as Kathleen Scott, on 9 February 1921:

> '. . . we had fun dressing him up in his Arabian clothes in the drawing-room, praying that my primmest aunt wouldn't be announced.'

That caveat certainly applied to the resultant life-sized bronze of a naked Lawrence, as he throws back his head and stretches out his arms with the palms open and upwards. Lawrence was equally happy to sit for portrait painters and book illustrators, notably Sir William Rothenstein:

> 'Generous with his time, he never seemed to object to

standing for hours together — once, when I was painting the folds of his outer garment, he remained standing for two hours without a rest.'

Perhaps missing the comradeship of conflict, or the adrenaline of war, Lawrence did the most bizarre thing for a high-ranking officer, by changing his name and re-entering the military in the lowest of ranks. The 'mind-suicide' of enlistment, as Lawrence called it, was partially explained by David Garnett:

'There are rational and logical explanations why Lawrence enlisted, but the final and most compelling explanation was an irrational urge to submit and subject himself to men most obviously his inferiors.'

William Roberts's portrait of Aircraftman John Hume Ross of the Royal Air Force in 1922

No one was happy about it. The War Office resisted and fellow officers regarded it as an embarrassment verging on madness. Colonial Secretary Winston Churchill did not want Lawrence to leave the Arab Affairs desk of the Middle East division of the Colonial Office. Churchill refused to accept Lawrence's resignation until he threatened to do something utterly stupid (allegedly to raise a brigade for Irish leader Michael Collins and attack Ulster).

The next to receive Lawrence's attention was his former associate Air Chief Marshal Sir Hugh Trenchard who was Chief of the Air Staff. He ordered that Lawrence was to be secretly allowed into the Royal Air Force as an Aircraftman under the assumed name John Hume Ross. When Lawrence presented himself for medical examination he was visibly malnourished and bore scars of recent beatings that were apparently self-inflicted. Captain William Earl Johns — the creator of gung-ho story book hero Biggles — had to find a civilian doctor to produce the necessary certificate after service doctors declined. Johns, under his own by-line in an article for the *Sunday Times* in 1957, recalled being told by his Commanding Officer:

'Watch your step. This man is Lawrence of Arabia. Get him in, or you'll get your bowler hat.'

Air Marshal Trenchard soon regretted allowing Lawrence into the RAF. Of all places, he was posted as a raw recruit to the Headquarters Depot on the outskirts of London. Hillingdon House at Uxbridge held the headquarters staff of the Air Defence of the United Kingdom. Notes of his experiences there became the autobiographical manuscript entitled *The Mint* which was published posthumously. No. 352087 Aircraftman 2 Ross, moved on to B.3 Block of the School of Photography at South Farnborough, Hampshire.

Lawrence of the Tank Corps at Bovington Camp, outside hut F-12, in 1923.

The most famous officer hero of the Great War re-entered the services from the bottom which was where he now intended to stay.

The inevitable happened, after Christmas in 1922, with exposés in the *Daily Express* and *Daily News*. Having 'the only white man ever made a Prince of Mecca' at Uxbridge and then Farnborough guaranteed that senior officers would have to run the gauntlet of the press pack at the gate in order to reach their desks. It took just four months from recruitment to civvy street.

Thrown out of the RAF, Lawrence used contacts and blackmail to try again elsewhere in the services. George Bernard Shaw's wife, Charlotte, relayed to Winston Churchill her fear that if he was thwarted again, he might commit suicide. This time he was spirited back into the ranks as Trooper Thomas Edward Shaw – a tribute to GBS – of the Tank Corps and posted to 'B' Company of its 1st (Depot) Battalion at Bovington Camp in the middle of the Dorset heath, between Wool and Bere Regis. On 18 October 1923, by King George V's warrant, the Corps became the Royal Tank Corps. By then, Lawrence was finding it anything but royal:

'The Army is muck, stink, and a desolate abomination.'

Fellow recruits in 'B' Company of 1st Depot Battalion of the Tank Corps were 'the sort who'd always throw something at any cat they saw'. Bovington was known as Tintown and Lawrence was billeted in one of those wooden sheds with a corrugated iron roof – Hut F-12 in Marcelcave Road (which now lies under the north-east wing of the 1938-built Sandhurst Barrack Block). Private T. E. Shaw's Army number was 7875698. He gave his personal address as 'Mr T. E. Shaw, care of H. Smith (Stationer), Bovington Camp, Wool, Dorset.'

The inner turmoil in Lawrence's life turned into the creative imperative for a literary record of the Desert Revolt. *The Seven Pillars of Wisdom*, a quote from the tenets of Islam, turned into an epic in the style of Homer and Virgil, burnished with touches of Charles Montagu Doughty's classic *Travels in Arabia Deserta*. A privately-produced edition of eight copies was printed and bound for him at the *Oxford Times* works in the summer of 1922. Its 'S. A.' dedication, if not to donkey-boy

> *Lawrence had established himself as the most quotable of our national heroes which, conversely, makes him the most inexplicable for us to explain.*

Bovington Camp in Dorset
used to be known as 'Tintown'.

Dahoum — using his proper initials — might be Sharif Ali ibn al-Hussein, given command of the Bedouin expedition against the Yarmuk viaduct, or even a combination of Dahoum and Sharif Ali, if one follows Desmond Stewart's logic in his biography of Lawrence, in 'the kind of involved sense that fits a cipher and fitted Lawrence'.

For a time, Lawrence was proactive in marketing the book, going with top London literary agent Raymond Savage to see young film-maker Herbert Wilcox who began his career with *Good Night Vienna*:

> the army is dyeing me khaki by degrees, + I don't know that I'm any longer much company for real people. At least I feel that way, so shall abstain till I'm different.

Lawrence's condemnation of Bovington life
in a letter to Sydney Cockerell.

'In a hesitant voice, which became stronger and deeper as he went along the author gave me an outline of his book which I found extremely interesting, but not good cinema and in spots rather sordid. In particular he told me of the . . . advances of a Turkish chief and how in desperation one night he fought him off with what he called "a knee kick", and the author being scourged and tortured for his attack. Since he was a British subject, masquerading as an Arab, which language he spoke like a native, his greatest fear was that during the torture he would cry out in English and not Arabic.'

To Wilcox, this was not entertainment which would attract movie-goers, but both agent and author strongly disagreed:

'Lawrence told me that one day it would make an out-standing film. He failed to sway me, but how right he was.'

One of Lawrence's first excursions on a motor-cycle into Dorset life, arranged for him by Robert Graves, was to meet Mr and Mrs Thomas Hardy at Max Gate, Dorchester, on Thursday 29 March 1923. They were to become pivotal in Lawrence's literary and social life. He described for Graves the 'dignity and ripeness' of a thoughtful recluse 'waiting so tranquilly for death' in 'that strange house hidden behind its thicket of trees'. His first impressions were imparted to Eric Kennington:

'I saw Hardy yesterday, paid for seeing him too, for it meant cutting a parade! However it was worth it, and I'm going again, if ever he asks me. His weakness in character-drawing is a reflection of himself. A very sensitive little man: faded now: with hope yet that mankind will give up warfare. He felt incredibly old to me.'

The next visit was on Saturday 26 May 1923. The poet and novelist Walter de la Mare was staying with the Hardys. He recalled in a radio broadcast in 1955 that Hardy had teased him that a prince was coming to tea, and he ran through a complete list of the royal family, dismissing each in turn. He remained on tenterhooks:

> 'Round about four came a ring at the bell. And as if a Jinni [evil fiery spirit of Mohammeden folklore] *had trumpeted in my ear, I realised that on the doorstep was Colonel Lawrence. And Colonel Lawrence, of course, was a Prince of Mecca.'*

On 3 June 1923, Lawrence made his excuses for not visiting, in a note dropped through the door at Max Gate, and rode to Plymouth for Private Butler to see his folks. The house guests at Max Gate were the caricaturist Max Beerbohm and Mr and Mrs Bernard Shaw. Lawrence regarded Beerbohm (along with Hilaire Belloc) as contemptibly light-weight but much admired Shaw, to the extent of having adopted his name. Private Butler probably had his charms and Lawrence expressed concern that he would be uncomfortable in such literary company. The following day, incidentally, was Thomas Hardy's 83rd birthday.

The next visit progressed inside the door on Sunday 29 July 1923 – following negotiations with Wessex the terrier – when the house guests were war poet Siegfried Sassoon and literary critic Edmund Blunden. Lawrence left Blunden with provocative memories. Having described Hardy's novels as poor, apart from their descriptive passages, and failing to recognise a 'home-grown quality' in the verses, he did admit to astonishment at the spectacle of Hardy the poet at such an advanced age.

> 'Something extraordinary always happens to that man.' – Charlotte Shaw about Lawrence, to husband George Bernard Shaw.

> 'I never saw him relax. He was surely a man with "ants in his pants".' – Corporal Alec Dixon of the Tank Corps.

*Clockwise from top left: The hillside from the cottage;
Clouds Hill as Lawrence knew it; The road out of
Bovington towards Clouds Hill where the next building
was a mile away; The cottage from the hillside;
Approaching Clouds Hill along the garden path.*

Life at Clouds Hill

Lawrence and Clouds Hill have been synonymous since September 1923. Having come across the 1808-built former gamekeeper's cottage in a rhododendron clump, standing in splendid isolation as the first building on the other side of the heath a mile north of the camp, he set about arranging to rent it from his cousin Harry Rupert Fetherstonhaugh-Frampton of Frampton House for half-a-crown per week (2 shillings 6 pence). The Framptons were notorious in Dorset — just inside living memory — for having been headed by the principal persecutor of the Tolpuddle Martyrs. Rising to 225 feet above sea level, Clouds Hill overlooked the Tank Park outside Tintown to which rusting hulks had been brought back from the

Fireplace in the main room downstairs at Clouds Hill.

Western Front. This far-away extremity of their land, in the heathland parish of Turners Puddle, was henceforth the shrine to Lawrence of Arabia. In his words, there was:

'Dorsetshire to look at ... In my cottage is no food and no bed. At nightfall there is a flea bag and I lie on the preferred patch of floor in either room. The ground room is for books, and the stair room is for music: music being the trade name for a gramophone and records. There are five acres of rhododendrons and fires every evening from the sticks.'

The bulky manuscript of *The Seven Pillars of Wisdom* was still with Charlotte and George Bernard Shaw that September, a year after Lawrence had sent it to them, without any substantive feedback by the time he moved into Clouds Hills. In fairness to GBS, he had made it clear that he hardly had time to read the daily paper, 'much less 300,000 words' (460,000, actually). Lawrence was also seeking advice from Charles Doughty, E. M. Forster, David and Edward Garnett (who cut it to 150,000 words), Florence and Thomas Hardy, David Hogarth and Siegfried Sassoon. Eric Kennington was asked to provide a mix of 'imaginative' and 'comic' cartoon-style drawings. Lawrence explained the underlying objective to Florence Hardy:

> 'It is meant to be the true history of a political movement whose essence was a fraud, in the sense that its leaders did not believe the arguments with which they moved its rank and file: and also the true history of a campaign, to show how unlovely the back of a commander's mind must be.'

Bernard Shaw procrastinated from the start, writing on 1 December 1922 :

Confinement in Dorset seems to have been vital for the final effort that saw The Seven Pillars of Wisdom *into print.*

> 'Patience, patience: do not again shoot your willing camel through the head. The truth is that I haven't read it yet.'

That still applied when Sassoon gave him an encouraging assessment in November 1923:

> 'Damn you, how long do you expect me to go on reassuring you about your bloody masterpiece: it is a GREAT BOOK, blast you. Are you satisfied?, you tank-vestigating eremite.'

'Nothing matters' or 'Does not care' are loose translations of Lawrence's Greek carving – from the story of Hippocleides in Herodotus – which he set above the door at Clouds Hill.

In the event, as 30 guinea cheques were 'rolling in merrily' for 128 subscription copies during 1924, George Bernard Shaw eventually responded but with a raft of changes. He instructed Lawrence to delete the opening chapter, re-write various supposed libels, and generally fussed about every colon and semi-colon.

In the one pleasure which Lawrence allowed himself, in public, he challenged Dorset's relatively primitive highways with high-speed transit on one of the world's most powerful motor-cycles ('the paragon of everything on wheels'). Corporal Alec Dixon was the pillion passenger at 83 miles per hour, through blinding rain, on the straight road between Blandford and Salisbury. This gave rise to Lawrence's Tank Corps' nickname which was 'Broughie' Shaw. Adrenaline flowed, as he confirmed to Lionel Curtis, in 1923:

'When my mood gets too hot and I find myself wandering beyond control I pull out my motor-bike and hurl it at top-speed through these unfit roads for hour after hour.'

Lawrence turned down the offer of spending Christmas with 'the Thomas Hardys' in 1923, writing to Florence that his 'ancient and splendid bicycle' had been borrowed and wrecked, which left him without transport. To Sydney Cockerell, however, he was doing 'rations and coalyard' duties at Bovington so that others could be 'free for their orgy' and added:

'It is not good to be too happy often.'

There was free time to be 'alone in my new-old cottage', he told R. M. Guy, for 'a quiet time of simply thinking'. By 30 December, however, he had been persuaded to attend Max Gate for lunch and share the afternoon with the Bernard Shaws. There was an appropriately Shavian welcome:

'Private Shaw meets Public Shaw.'

It was none of that nonsense for the Hardys. Florence insisted upon addressing him, properly, as 'Colonel Lawrence'. Thomas said that he would be proud of such a rank. No thoughts for him of a belittling Private Hardy. To Thomas Hardy, the French Wars were the First World War, and Lawrence reflected on the half-century disconnect between their lives and times:

'Napoleon is a real man to him and the county of Dorsetshire echoes that name everywhere in Hardy's ears. He lives in his period, and thinks of it as the Great War; whereas to me that nightmare through the fringe of which I had passed has dwarfed all memories of other wars, so that they seem trivial, half-amusing incidents.'

Edward Morgan Forster (1879-1970), who had just published *Aspects of the Novel*, was the house guest at Max Gate when Lawrence called on Sunday 30 March 1924. When E. M. Forster returned to Dorset, on Friday 20 June 1924 for the weekend, he stayed at Clouds Hill.

Lawrence ran the quartermaster's stores at Bovington as 'a sort of half clerk, half storeman' for two years.

Siegfried Sassoon and T. E. Lawrence were visitors to the Hardys on 6 August 1924 when they arranged a joint outing on the 28th, to hear the operatic version of Thomas Hardy's last play, *Iseult, or the Famous Tragedy of the Queen of Cornwall*, produced by composer Rutland Boughton on a Wagnerian scale in the ruins of Glastonbury Abbey, which he turned into a British Bayreuth. Lawrence left his motor-cycle at Dorchester and they went together by car. E. M. Forster also joined them. Their return went into Max Gate folklore as the night when Hardy pointedly removed burning coal from the fire to save it for another day.

Lawrence claimed to have seen the Hardys every Sunday in 1925. He was invited by Florence to edit her husband's diary for publication, but as with an offer from Sir Hugh Trenchard the previous year — to write the official history of the Royal Flying Corps in the Great War — Lawrence either turned down the assignment or let the matter drop.

Hardy could forget the thread of current conversation, but had total recall as a 6-year-old, seeing Scots Greys in a public house in Dorchester, and becoming intoxicated from the beer fumes. Lawrence revelled in all-male company. He could see no beauty or interest in the female form and asked artist Eric Kennington:

'Do you really like naked women? They express so little.'

He displayed studied indifference to the erotic piles of work in progress — or rejected — in the Alderney, Poole, studio of Bohemian portrait painter Augustus John. To Sydney Cockerell he confirmed not only feeling frigid towards women but equally uninterested in their minds and specifically that of one popular poet:

'No I haven't heard of Charlotte Mew: but all the women who ever wrote original stuff could have been strangled at birth, and the history of English literature (and my bookshelves) would be unchanged …'

Cockerell persevered in singing her praises, as poor Charlotte went on to kill herself by swallowing disinfectant, but Lawrence maintained his distance from the verse of 'a real poet … but a little one':

Lawrence the misogynist, demolishing tragic poet Charlotte Mew.

'I'm frigid towards women, so that I can withstand her: so that I want to withstand her.'

His excuse to Robert Graves was that the military life removed all opportunity:

'Being a mechanic cuts one off from all real communication towards women.'

Privates Alec Dixon and Posh Palmer were the first regulars at Clouds Hill. Visitors tended to be the young admired.

An Eric Kennington cartoon of Lawrence, shown at eye-level with his mantelpiece and grasping a tin of beans, is captioned 'Haute cuisine'. Thomas Hardy's maid, Nellie Titterington, used to treat

'Haute cuisine' – Eric Kennington's cartoon of Lawrence.

"HAUTE CUISINE"

Lawrence to a cup of Bovril before he motor-cycled home from the author's home at Max Gate. The sparse dietary situation at Clouds Hill was recalled by E. M. Forster in a wireless broadcast in 1938:

'We drank water only or tea – no alcohol ever entered Clouds Hill – and we ate … this sounds less romantic … out of tins.'

Corporal Alec Dixon, from Bovington Camp, described a typical Clouds Hill gathering:

'TE was an expert in "mixed grills" where men were concerned. He presided over the company, settling arguments, patiently answering all manner of questions, feeding the gramophone, making tea, stoking the fire, and by some magic of his own, managing to keep everyone in good humour. There were many picnic meals (stuffed olives, salted almonds, and Heinz baked beans were regular features) washed down with TE's own blend of

Gramophone in the music room upstairs at Clouds Hill photographed by Colin Graham.

China tea. Some of us used chairs, others the floor, while TE always ate standing up by the end of the wide oak mantel-shelf which had been fitted at a [low] height convenient for him.'

The evidence of Bovington's shopkeepers, however, is that Lawrence — when alone — was an ordinary omnivore. F. J. Stratton, the butcher opposite the Post Office, regularly sold him 'two chops for his lunch'. Mr and Mrs H. White, fishmongers, told Wareham historian Harry Broughton that he was partial to fish and chips and finnan haddock. The latter was bought for Lawrence by 'old Mrs Knowles', the mother of his neighbour, Pat Knowles. When Lawrence came into the shop he would never join a queue. So Mrs White instantly made up a parcel of fish and chips as if he had ordered them in advance.

Lawrence's pair of leather zip-beds were named Meum and Teum (with the latter being stolen after the Panavision film appeared).

Desperate to leave Bovington Camp and rejoin the Royal Air Force, in the spring of 1924, he persuaded Air Chief Marshal Trenchard to agree, but this was blocked by Samuel Hoare as Secretary of State for Air. Lawrence turned to John Buchan, Director of Information at the end of the Great War and the author of *The Thirty-Nine Steps*, to use his influence with Prime Minister Stanley Baldwin. Then Lawrence used his trump card of emotional blackmail. Either he would have his own way or take his life, with this threat to Edward Garnett on 13 June 1924:

'I'm no bloody good on earth. So I'm going to quit: but in my usual comic fashion. I'm going to finish the reprint [of Seven Pillars] and square up with [Jonathan] Cape before I hop it. There is nothing like deliberation, order and regularity in these things. I shall bequeath my notes on life in the recruits camp of the RAF [his manuscript of The Mint]. They will disappoint you.'

Garnett relayed the ultimatum to George Bernard Shaw who in turn warned the Prime Minister of the prospect of 'an appalling scandal' particularly as publication of Lowell Thomas's *With Lawrence in Arabia* had revived the Prince of Mecca legend. Against their better judgment, Hoare and Trenchard capitulated to Lawrence's infuriatingly frequent demands. After riding recklessly back from the RAF college at Cranwell to Clouds Hill — at 108 miles per hour — Lawrence wrote to Francis Rodd that his decision had been to make his exit at Christmas. Instead, when it came around, he was toasting Stanley Baldwin and John Buchan as he planned his next adventure.

In August 1925, when he was at the RAF Cadet College, Cranwell, motor-cycle manufacturer George Brough gave Lawrence the news his latest SS 110 model for 1926 was ready for collection, from his Nottingham works. This he

Lawrence the biker on Brough Superior RK 4907.

called George V — his fifth Brough Superior since 1922 — and despite having skidded on ice and crashed in December 1925 ('Hobble like a cripple now') it was on this machine that Lawrence completed 100,000 miles of riding on 26 September 1926. He wrote a promotional puff for Brough's stand at Olympia:

'Your present machines are as fast and reliable as express trains, and the greatest fun in the world to drive ... The SS. 100 holds the road extraordinarily. It's my great game on a pot-holed road to open up to 70 mph or so and feel the machine gallop: and though only a touring machine it will do 90 mph at full throttle.'

While at Cranwell, from September 1925 to November 1926, Lawrence made arrangements for 'a room in some near village' to 'begin work'. He paid 2 shillings a day (from his 3 shillings a day RAF pay) to Miss Ruby Bryant of 31 Portland Street, Newark.

Back in Bovington, with Corporal Alec Dixon, Lawrence handed back the keys of a room in Woodside Cottage, Bovington, which they had been renting from camp hairdresser J. F. Forse. It was stuffed with drawings, manuscripts and notes including material apparently from

On his fifth Brough in 1925.

Seven Pillars. Lawrence had admitted to Florence Hardy that he had been 'suppressing the book'. Forse eventually consigned 'three or four tea-chests full' to the bonfire though both his father, J. W. Forse and assistant, Miss Read, had taken some papers and illustrations. Mr Forse provided details

to the *Dorset County Chronicle* a decade later and lamented:

'I realise now I was burning money.'

From November 1926, Lawrence then arranged payment of 6 pence a day to W. J. Ross of 76 Marsham Street, Westminster, and 9 pence a day went to Jock Bruce, his bodyguard, from his first Tank Corps days. Thanks to his benign banker, foxhunter Robin Buxton, his finances were allowed to bump along the bottom with a £7,000 overdraft.

In his investment for life Lawrence acquired the freehold of Clouds Hill from the Frampton Estate for £450 in 1929.

India and Speedboats

Lawrence arranged a transfer to India in December 1926. Arriving on the troopship HMT *Derbyshire*, he reported to the Engine Repair Shops at the Aircraft Depot in Drigh Road, Karachi. From there he was transferred inland to 20 (Army Co-Operation) Squadron which flew Bristol Fighters from Peshawar. Then he went to Miranshah Fort, Waziristan, in the tribal and troubled North-West Frontier District of pre-partition India. This was the smallest and most remote RAF station in India:

'... all ringed by mountains, and on the edge of Afghanistan ... We are not allowed beyond the barbed wire by day, or outside the fort walls by night.'

Aircraftman T. E. Shaw of the Royal Air Force posing for Flight-Lieutenant Stanley Smetham in Miranshah, India, in 1928.

While in India, Lawrence officially dropped his family name — or name of convenience to cover his late father's retreat from Chapman — and legally adopted that of Thomas Edward Shaw by deed poll.

Modestly describing himself as 'the only airman who can work a typewriter' he was out of the country and far away but this inevitably led to media speculation.

The *New York World* received a report in July 1928, claiming he had gone on a 'Mysterious Mission' across Persia, dressed as an Arab sheikh, to negotiate with Riza Khan. That sounded just plausible —

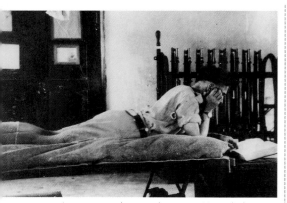

*Lawrence in the guard-room at Miranshah,
beside a rack of rifles, in 1928.*

derlands. The story spread back to London that Lawrence was responsible for the troubles of Amanullah Khan, the Amir of Afghanistan, whose reforms triggered a rebellion. The official Kabul newspaper *Amany Afghan* was unconvinced:

> 'We do not believe in Colonel Lawrence's power and skill. He is only an Englishman.'

Amanullah was forced to abdicate and fled to Rome. Meantime, Lawrence had been ordered home, flying from Miranshah to Lahore on 8 January 1929, and there to Karachi the following day. He boarded the SS *Rajputana* at Bombay and sailed for Tilbury on 12 January. Wing Commander Sydney Smith came alongside the ship off Plymouth and told Lawrence that he was now based there, in the flying-boat base at RAF Cattewater (which was being renamed Mount Batten). It was an instant start for a firm friendship.

Plymouth reporter James Judge met Lawrence at Lady Astor's local residence in Elliot Terrace and wrote to disassociate

and might have been published — but the same report had Lawrence continuing his travels through Arabia, to detach the Yemen from Italy, and sort out local difficulties in Aden. It was spiked. The Berlin newspapers were less constrained. 'The world's arch-spy' was up to his old tricks in the next chapter of the 'Great Game' across those perpetually insecure bor-

himself from a report in the *Morning News*. It drew this response from Lawrence on 5 May 1929:

> *'I've never publicly acknowledged or denied anything published about me.'*

Cattewater rewarded him with two boy-toys that were almost as much fun as his Brough motor-cycle. The first was a civilian Moth seaplane (registration G-EBYV) in which as pilot he whisked Major A. A. Nathan around on a tour of the western estuaries, the Scilly Isles and the Channel Islands. Major Colin Cooper then loaned him an American-made Purdy Biscayne Baby speedboat — *The Biscuit* — as he was introduced to the project to create an equivalent British all-weather high speed launch.

Lawrence helped Wing Commander Smith manage the Schneider Cup sea-plane races over the Solent in 1929. He notoriously upstaged Lord Thomson in the media stakes when the Minister for Air in the new Labour administration naively asked why he was sweeping a slipway for Italian competitors. This time Lawrence narrowly kept what was developing into what others might regard as his first real job. When he heard that Lord Thomson had been killed in the inferno that destroyed the *R101* airship, in October 1930, there was a domestic interlude as Lawrence's mother visited Clouds Hill. Acting like an 'enraged housewife' she 'remorselessly' cleaned the cottage.

Seaplanes and launches took part in exercises at Plymouth in November 1930 to improve upon air-sea rescue techniques. In the process one of the aircraft began to sink and Lawrence dived into the water to secure a hawser around the hull. While stationed at Mount Batten, at 11.30 hours on 4 February 1931, Aircraftman 338171 Shaw witnessed the landing of Blackburn Iris flying-boat S238, literally into Plymouth Sound.

The wings of the biplane folded back and 'the hull dived straight to the bottom', taking Wing Commander Charles Tucker and eight others to their deaths. It transpired that

Tucker — as commanding officer — had pulled rank to take over the controls from the pilot. Through his influence with Nancy Astor, who conveniently sat as a Plymouth Member of Parliament, Lawrence had the law changed to adopt the maritime rule that prevents use of seniority in such situations.

In 1931, Lawrence produced the most precise piece of writing of his life with what David Garnett hailed as 'a masterpiece of technology'. The 80-page foolscap work was entitled *Notes on Handling the 200 Class Seaplane Tender*. At the same time he was providing inspiration and input for at least one-and-a-half characters in George Bernard Shaw's latest play *Too Good to be True* based on post-war service life.

While seconded to the British Power Boat Company at Hythe on Southampton Water, for long periods from 1931 to 1933, Lawrence liaised with RAF units on practical problems with engines ranging from oil pressure valves to toggle collars. Delivering boats and instructing crews, he described himself as 'part mechanic, part water-chauffeur'. The Hythe company

designed and constructed *Miss England* which (at 92.8 miles per hour) held the official record as the fastest single-engine boat in the world. When they were testing it in the Solent, Lawrence took lodgings at 119 Clarence Road, East Cowes, on the Isle of Wight. His other temporary address was 13 Birmingham Street, Southampton.

In September 1933, in a letter to Flight-Sergeant Clarke at his old base, Mount Batten, Lawrence asked if his copies of D. H. Lawrence's *Letters* and *War Birds* had been found as he was 'spending money on my cottage' and all his books were now at Clouds Hill. On her visit to Lawrence in his Dorset retreat, his mother had attempted bringing a touch of domesticity by treating it as an ordinary garden, but in 1933 Lawrence declared he had given away or otherwise exterminated all traces of her planting scheme:

'Clouds Hill is no place for tame flowers.'

Against Lawrence's wishes, his ageing mother and brother Bob were planning to return to China, to a Christian mission. By the end of the year, Lawrence had eight new 37.5-feet launches on various trials, including one provided as a high-speed pinnace for 'the Chief of Staff, Portsmouth Dockyard'. He signed off a technical letter ('About the toggle-collar') to Flight-Sergeant Clarke on 24 November with a motor-cycling up-date:

'The old bike is running like a new one.'

What Lowell Thomas had done for Lawrence in film, and Robert Graves with words in *Lawrence and the Arabs*, was repeated when respected military historian Basil Liddell Hart published his biography in the spring of 1934. It idolised and lionised Lawrence, who posed for a publicity photograph with the author, standing on a quayside capstan at Hythe (so that both were of equal height).

Lawrence's last two published letters, from 7 and 8 May 1935, include typically mysterious and poignant remarks. The puzzle, which can be read as a premonition, was to K. W. Marshall, in answer to whether he had yet had a chance to read *Daughters of Albion* by Alec Brown:

'Thank them for the Brown monster. I have not tackled it yet. The noble weather and various causes have kept me outdoors from dawn till dark, and sent me dead-beat to bed immediately it was decent to sleep. But that ceases in ten days.'

He also turned down a potential job offers from Lady Astor and suggestions to join her Cliveden Set which included several of Lawrence's closest friends (notably Lord 'Eddie' Winterton and Geoffrey Dawson who lost the editorship of *The Times* for advocating German appeasement).

'No: wild mares would not at present take me away from Clouds Hill. It is an earthly paradise and I am staying here till I feel qualified for it. Also there is something broken in the works, as I told you: my will I think. In this mood I would not take on any job at all. So do not commit *yourself to advocating me, lest I prove a non-starter.'*

His final four months in the services were at the harbour-side in RAF Bridlington, North Humberside, providing target boats for an offshore bombing range, ending on 26 February 1935. He was photographed leaving on a pedal-cycle. 'Damn the press,' Lawrence wrote as he headed south through London, but the problem, as Lowell Thomas put it, was his own knack for 'backing into the limelight'. He wrote to John Buchan on 1 April 1935:

'My life? Not too good. The press were besetting this cottage when I reached it. I went to London for a while: they desisted.'

Lawrence made personal protests to the Press Association and Newspaper Proprietors' Association, which was followed by direct action with his

Lawrence on his bike, photographed by Ian Deheer, leaving RAF Bridlington in March 1935.

housekeeper, Pat Knowles. 'Come on Pat, let's be rid of them,' he said as an intruding cameraman was punched in the eye and thrown out of the garden. Lawrence's anger was followed by shock as he held his head in his hand:

'It's years since I hit a man.'

Lawrence's last letter to Eric Kennington was written on 6 May 1935 which was the night of King George V's silver jubilee with celebratory bonfires flickering across Dorset's night sky:

'Days seem to dawn, suns to shine, evenings to follow, and I to sleep. What have I done, what am I doing, what am I going to do, puzzle me and bewilder me. Have you ever been a leaf and fallen from your tree in autumn and been really puzzled by it?'

Death Leaves its Mysteries

Was Lawrence in a state of 'despondency' after retiring from the RAF, as his brother Arnold believed, or was he preparing for a new role in life? Colonel Richard Meinertzhagen's *Middle East Diary*, held as a manuscript in Rhodes House Library, Oxford, claims that in May 1935 Lawrence was chairing a review panel considering the restructuring of Britain's entire secret security services:

'We worked together in the CO [Colonial Office] on a scheme for a Directorship of Intelligence embracing both political and military aspects and coalescing under one head, FO [Foreign Office], WO [War Office] Admiralty, Air Ministry, Scotland Yard. Put the thing to Churchill, Amery, Macdonogh, they concurred. *Involved training college in London and one in the country. It was complete and we were applying for Treasury sanction when TE died. I felt I could not go on with it as it was very much his work.'*

Lawrence on GW 2275, his final
motor-cycle, beside the
rhododendrons at Clouds Hill.

Winston Churchill always maintained that, had he lived, Lawrence would have played a leading role in the coming conflict. The other two had long shadowed the intelligence community. Leopold Stennett Amery (1873-1955) was Assistant Secretary to the War Cabinet in 1917 and a post-war Colonial Secretary. Lieutenant-General Sir George Macdonogh (1865-1942) had been the wartime Director of Military Intelligence.

The road traffic accident that killed T. E. Lawrence took place as he was riding back to Clouds Hill after sending a telegram from the Post Office at Bovington Camp to the author Henry Williamson on 13 May 1935. Lawrence had visited Williamson in Georgeham, Devon, after he had won the Hawthornden Prize for *Tarka the Otter* in 1928. In 1935, before becoming the intellectual guru for Sir Oswald Mosley's British Union of Fascists (painting its lightning-flash emblem on his house and car) Williamson on his own initiative planned sending Lawrence as a peace envoy to meet Hitler in Germany. They would then call a mass meeting of fellow ex-servicemen of the Great War to fill the Albert Hall. Williamson saw in Hitler a beam of hope for the future and claimed that Lawrence shared his vision:

'He read the speeches of Hitler, and was confirmed in his divination. A man who had served in the ranks of the infantry, been wounded, and blinded by mustard gas, a man who loved Beethoven and lived only for the res-urrection of his country's happiness — a nation's honour —

a man who was the ideal of youth, was one who not only knew the truth, but could speak it and convey it to the minds of others. He was a corner-stone for the new, realistic pacification of Europe.'

Williamson regarded Hitler ('the great man across the Rhine') and Lawrence as 'prophets of peace'. He championed a 'whirlwind campaign' for a resurgent Europe:

'The new age must begin — England was ready for peace. Lawrence was the natural leader of that age in England. I dreamed of an Anglo-German friendship, the beginning of the pacification of Europe. Hitler and Lawrence must meet. I wrote this to him.'

Lawrence's telegram on 13 May confirmed he was prepared to discuss the possibilities with Williamson:

'Lunch Tuesday Wet Fine Cottage One Mile North Bovington Camp.'

Clockwise from top left: Present-day view of the crash site, after wartime road widening, beneath the closest pair of cyclists; A butcher's bike, ridden by Albert Hargraves, was hit by Lawrence's motor-cycle; Crown Hill Camp, beside which Lawrence fell from his motorcycle on 13 May 1935; Lawrence's motorcycle, after the crash; Daily Sketch photograph of the crash site, looking north along the road towards Clouds Hill.

Coming home from Bovington, 450 yards from his cottage at 11.20 am, Lawrence was on Brough Superior GW 2275 which he called *George VII*. He was moving at 50 to 60 mph as he came up and over the brow of a low rise on a road that was then much narrower than it has been since the Second World War. It was a straight stretch of unfenced carriageway, approaching the pine trees of Moreton Plantation on the left side where a sandy path joined from the heath. Opposite there was a water-tank and the military tents of Crown Hill Camp. The only adult witness who gave evidence at the inquest, Corporal Ernest Catchpole of the Royal Army Ordnance Corps from Tidworth, said he had seen a black car 'not going very fast' coming from the Clouds Hill direction, that passed Lawrence just before the crash.

Forty-six-year-old Lawrence swerved at this moment to avoid two boy cyclists, butcher's errand boy Albert Hargraves (14) and his friend Frank Fletcher. Hitting Bert's rear wheel, knocking him off and throwing the cycle into Frank who was also knocked off, Lawrence and his motor-cycle slid along the road. Both Bert and Lawrence were injured and taken to Bovington Military Hospital. The reporter for the *Dorset County Chronicle* commented:

> 'Those who knew Lawrence knew such a brilliant motor-cyclist, even though he was travelling at 50 or 60 mph would never crash aimlessly into a cyclist unless he was faced with a last second difficulty in his path.'

Albert Hargraves made a full recovery but Lawrence never regained consciousness. He died at Bovington on 19 May 1935 from 'congestion of the lungs and heart failure following a fracture of the skull and laceration of the brain'. Viscount Allenby broadcast to the nation that day:

> 'In T. E. Shaw, better known to the public as Colonel T. E. Lawrence, I have lost a good friend and valued comrade. When first I met him — in the summer of 1917 — he had just returned from a venturesome raid behind the Turkish front. Thenceforth, until the Armistice, we were closely

associated in the conduct of the campaigns of 1917 and 1918 in Palestine and Syria — closely, that is, in mind and purpose, though distance often separated us widely.

'Lawrence was under my command, but after acquainting him with my strategic plan, I gave him a free hand. His co-operation was marked by the utmost loyalty, and I never had anything but praise for his work, which, indeed was invaluable throughout the campaign.

'He was the mainspring of the Arab movement. He knew the language, their manners, their mentality; he understood their merry, sly humour; in daring, he led them; in endurance he equalled, if not surpassed, their strongest. Though in complete sympathy with his companions, and sharing to the full with them hardship and danger, he was careful to maintain the dignity of his position as Confidential Advisor to the Emperor Feisal. Himself an Emir, he wore the robes of that rank, and kept up a suitable degree of state.

'His own bodyguard — men of wild and adventurous spirit — were all picked by Lawrence personally. Mounted on thoroughbred camels, they followed him in all his daring rides; and among those reckless desert rangers there was none who would not willingly have died for their chief. In fact, not a few lost their lives through devotion to him and in defence of his person. The shy and retiring scholar, archaeologist, philosopher, was swept by war into a position undreamed of.

'His well-balanced brain and disciplined imagination facilitated adaptation to the new environment; and there shone forth a brilliant tactician, with a genius for leadership. Such men win friends — such also find critics and detractors. But the highest reward for success is the inward knowledge that it has been rightly won. Praise or blame were regarded with indifference by Lawrence. He did his duty as he saw it before him. He has left, to us who knew and admired him, a beloved memory; and to all his countrymen, the example of a life well spent in the service.'

The inquest, held by the coroner for East Dorset, Major Ralph Neville Jones, returned a verdict of 'Accidental death' in the court-room at Bovington on the morning of Tuesday 21 May as Lawrence's body lay under a Union flag in the nearby mortuary chapel. That afternoon Winston Churchill led the mourners from the funeral service in St Nicholas Church, Moreton, around the corner beside the village school to the newly opened cemetery on the other side of the lane.

Top left: *Lawrence's coffin leaving Bovington Military Hospital for the funeral at Moreton.*
Top right: *Winston Churchill and wife Clementine walking up the drive to St Nicholas Church, Moreton, for Lawrence's funeral.*
Left: *Six pall-bearers with the bier – Aircraftman W. Bradbury; Arthur Russell from the Royal Tank Corps; illustrator Eric Kennington; local helper Pat Knowles; Colonel Stewart Newcombe RE from the Arab Revolt; Sir Ronald Storrs, wartime Governor of Jerusalem.*

Films and Monuments

There are memorials to T. E. Lawrence in Dorset, London and Oxford. His headstone is in Moreton village cemetery (with the Shaw name omitted). Clouds Hill, with 7.5 acres of land and selected memorabilia, was given to the National Trust by Arnold Lawrence in 1937 and appears on the map as Lawrence of Arabia's Cottage.

Eric Kennington's life-sized effigy in the robes of a Prince of Mecca reposes inside St Martin's Conquest-period church on Wareham's Saxon walls. The memorial in the capital is in St Paul's Cathedral, where his memorial service was held, with a bust by Eric

Lawrence's gravestone in Moreton Cemetery.

Kennington being placed in the Crypt. There are several memorials to him in Jesus College, Oxford, from a bronze plaque in the entrance to portraits in oils and pencil and a copy of the Kennington bust, in Jesus Chapel. The surviving siblings established the Lawrence Brothers Memorial Scholarship.

Alexander Korda had wanted to film *The Revolt in the Desert* — before Lawrence's death — with Robert Donat or Leslie Howard in the lead role. Lawrence wrote to both Charlotte Shaw and Bruce Rogers on 26 January 1935 that the project had been shelved as a result of a lunchtime discussion:

> 'No, there will be no Korda movie of me. The rumours grew thick, so I bearded the lion-maker and persuaded him to leave me alone.'

Henry Williamson records that the project was revived after Lawrence's death:

> 'At the bar of the Savage Club they were talking of difficulties in the making of the Lawrence of Arabia film. I wonder what, eventually, they will make of his life, for the public. His real-life struggle would be arresting and poignant; but they won't make that. The

Eric Kennington, Lawrence's book illustrator, who sculpted his bust and effigy.

Kennington's life-sized Lawrence, as a Prince of Mecca, in St Martin's Church, Wareham.

theme will be Lawrence of Arabia. Siegfried Sassoon was selected to write the scenario. It must have given him much discomposure.'

Another war interrupted such plans. The Rank Organisation, which held rights to *The Seven Pillars of Wisdom*, decided in the mid-1950s to approve £700,00 for its filming in Iraq. The Honourable Anthony 'Puffin' Asquith (1902-68) was commissioned as its producer. The younger son of the Liberal Prime Minister, he had produced several classic movies, including *The Winslow Boy*, *The Browning Version*, *The Young Lovers* and *Carrington VC*. He approached the actor Dirk Bogarde with a script by Terence Ratiggan on Lawrence and 'his still unexplained death on the lonely country road to Clouds Hill'. Frank Rattigan, the scriptwriter's father, had been a diplomat in Cairo and a friend of Ronald Storrs before the Great War. Bogarde enthused over the 'beautiful script':

'I had never, in my life, wanted a part, or script, so much.'

The project was pulled on 14 March 1958. It was 'my bitterest disappointment' for Dirk Bogarde who thought the Security Service might have stepped into 'a matter of politics' to prevent 'exposure of 'a very private man' ending his life in 'a forbidden area' with a 'lonely road, a black car, two school boys, skid marks'.

What caused the Rank Organisation to change its mind is more likely to be connected with the fact that their initiative coincided with strong competition from Hollywood. Producer Sam Spiegel — who had just won six Oscars with *Bridge on the River Kwai* — teamed up with ambitious director David Lean and commissioned a script from Robert

> *'I am not a very tractable person, much less of a hero-worshipper, but I could have followed Lawrence over the edge of the world. I loved him for himself, and also because there seemed to be reborn in him all the lost friends of my youth.'* — John Buchan (1875-1940), adventure writer and Lloyd-George's wartime Director of Information.

> *'What could be more extraordinary than the survival of this cult, which flourishes more as his lies and attitudinising are made manifest? He is superlatively a case of everything being true except the facts. What more fitting to be a Hero of Our Time than this, our English Genêt... with Lowell Thomas for his Sartre and Alec Guinness to say Amen?'* — Malcolm Muggeridge (1903-90), ex-Cairo lecturer, Intelligence Corps Major and international news correspondent.

'He is one of the few entirely satisfactory people
in the world. He can be so very kind.'
Florence Hardy (wife of author Thomas Hardy).

Bolt. This would turn into the Panavision spectacular *Lawrence of Arabia*, though with Peter O'Toole rather than Marlon Brando, Alec Guinness or Albert Finney (who were Spiegel's selections for the lead).

Rattigan salvaged parts of his script for a stage play, produced by Hugh Beaumont and starring Alec Guinness, which despite resistance opened as *Ross* in the Haymarket on 12 May 1960. Arnold Lawrence, as Lawrence's literary executor, asked Robert Graves to 'vet it for him and try to make it less disgusting'. He felt that if he and his 98-year-old mother objected strongly enough to the Lord Chamberlain they could 'stop the play altogether'. Graves thought Arnold Lawrence had successfully spiked it when he summed up the position for Karl Gay on 13 October 1959:

'So now he's written to tell Beaumont definitely that all is off. Beaumont has now tried to contact me to bring pressure, but I say that I'm in no state to be bullied and the affair is out of my hands ...

Arnold Lawrence also enlisted Robert Graves to monitor the Lean-Spiegel production to ensure that his brother emerged like a character from a Western-style movie rather than in a portrayal with 'psychological slants or libels'. Again, Graves promised to deliver, having already sold the film rights to *Lawrence and the Arabs* (with stage payments of £1,000 and £3,000) and also obtained £2,000 from the sale of

*Lawrence had the presence of an
extraordinary being who was outside the
jurisdiction of the world and remained strangely
untamed and untrammelled by convention –
to paraphrase Winston Churchill for whom
The Seven Pillars of Wisdom ranked with the
greatest books in the English language.*

manuscript letters. Graves wrote to Derek Savage on 7 December 1959:

> *'I probably would have got stuck like you in the rustic economy if T. E. Lawrence hadn't given me a helping hand, back in 1926; and curiously enough since his death there's always been something coming in from him to help me whenever things got tough.'*

In this age of the image, T. E. Lawrence has been transfigured into the handsome blue-eyed, fair hair form of Peter O'Toole. He has grown in stature in the process.

> *'Old age to him was pathetic. T. E. hoped not to live to grow old. That meant anything over 45.'* – illustrator and sculptor Eric Kennington.

Peter O'Toole starring in Lawrence of Arabia.

Bibliography

Aldington, Richard. *Lawrence of Arabia: A Biographical Enquiry.* (London, 1955).

Bogarde, Dirk. *Snakes and Ladders* (London, 1979).

Buchan, John. *Memory, Hold-the-Door* (London, 1940).

Dixon, Alec. *Tinned Soldier: a Personal Record, 1919-26* (London 1941).

Farson, Daniel. *Henry: An Appreciation of Henry Williamson* (London, 1982).

Garnett, David (Editor). *The Letters of T. E. Lawrence* (London, 1936).

Graves, Robert. *Lawrence and the Arabs* (London, 1927).

James, Lawrence. *The Golden Warrior* (London, 1990).

Kennet, Kathleen, Lady. *Self-portrait of an Artist: the Lady Kennet Diaries* (London, 1955).

Knightley, Phillip and Simpson, Colin. *The Secret Lives of Lawrence of Arabia* (London, 1969).

Lawrence, Arnold (Editor). *T. E. Lawrence by his Friends* (London, 1937).

Lawrence, Arnold (Editor). *Letters to T. E. Lawrence* (London, 1964 edition).

Legg, Rodney. *Lawrence of Dorset: From Arabia to Clouds Hill* (Wincanton, 2000).

Liddell Hart, Basil. *T. E. Lawrence: In Arabia and After* (London, 1934).

Mack, John E. *A Prince of Our Disorder: the Life of T. E. Lawrence* (New York, 1976).

Maugham, Robin. *Escape from the Shadows* (London, 1972).

Meinhertzhagen, Richard. *Middle East Diary: 1917-56* (London, 1959, with the original diaries being in Rhodes House Library, Oxford)

O'Prey, Paul. *Robert Graves: Between Moon and Moon, 1946-72* (London, 1990).

Richards, Vyvyan Warren. *Portrait of T. E. Lawrence: the Lawrence of The Seven Pillars of Wisdom* (London, 1936).

Sinclair, Andrew. *Spiegel: the Man behind the Pictures* (London 1987).

Stewart, Desmond. *T. E. Lawrence* (London, 1977).

Vansittart, Lord. *The Mist Procession* (London, 1958).

Wansell, Geoffrey. *Terence Rattigan* (London, 1995).

Ward, Bernard T. *Lawrence of Arabia & Pole Hill, Chingford* (Chingford Historical Society, 1976).

Wilcox, Herbert. *Twenty-five Thousand Sunsets: the Autobiography of Herbert Wilcox* (London, 1967).

Williamson, Henry. *Goodbye West Country* (London 1937).

Young, B. A. *The Rattigan Version* (London, 1986).